I0750874

[HOUSE BILL, No. 19.]

HOUSE OF REPRESENTATIVES.—January 27, 1863.—Read first and second times, referred to Committee on Quartermaster and Commissary Departments and Military Transportation, and ordered to be printed.

[By Mr. MILES.]

A BILL

To provide for the safe and expeditious transportation of troops and munitions of war by railroads.

SECTION 1. *The Congress of the Confederate States of America do enact,* That to facilitate the efficient, prompt, and uninterrupted transportation of troops and military munitions and supplies, the President shall appoint a Military Chief of Railroad Transportation, who shall have the rank of a Lieutenant Colonel and receive compensation at the rate of five thousand dollars per annum, payable quarterly, who shall hold his office during the pleasure of the President, and who shall be selected from the railroad officers in the Confederate States with a special view to his judgment, skill and experience in the practical details of railroad operations and machinery, and who shall hold no other office nor employment during its continuance.

SEC. 2. *Be it further enacted*, That the said Military Chief of Railroad Transportation shall be authorized and required to divide the railroads in the Confederate States into not less than two nor more than four Railroad Districts, over each of which districts the President shall appoint a District Military Superintendent, who shall have the rank of a Major, with the annual compensation of sixteen hundred dollars per annum, and who shall also be selected from the railroad officers of the Confederate States, with a special view to his judgment, experience and skill in the operations and machinery of railroads, and who shall hold his office at the pleasure of the President.

SEC. 3. *Be it further enacted*, That the acting President and Superintendent of each railroad shall, *ex officio*, be the local and special Military Superintendents of the operations of each such railroad, and shall have the rank, respectively, the President of a Major and the Superintendent of a Captain, but without any pay or pecuniary compensation to either by virtue of such rank.

SEC. 4. *Be it further enacted*, That the Road Master and each Conductor of Passenger trains, and other trains conveying troops, of each railroad, shall have the rank, but without any pay as such, of a First Lieutenant; and each Chief Station Agent and Section Master shall have the rank, but without any pay as such, of Second Lieutenant.

Sec. 5. *Be it further enacted,* That in all matters pertaining to their respective official duties as railroad officers and pertaining to railroad operations entrusted to their care, each of the officers of railroads herein named, shall have complete and exclusive control, and be subject to no interference or control of any military officer, of whatever rank, except as hereinafter provided for; and that any military officer, of whatever rank, not engaged in the management of any railroad, who shall interfere with the movement of any train or other operations of such road, shall be deemed guilty of a military offence, and, upon charges preferred by the President of the railroad company, may be tried and punished at the discretion of a court martial.

Sec. 6. *Be it further enacted,* That each such railroad officer shall, as to the operations of his railroad and the protection of its property, be clothed, according to his rank and within the scope of his duties, with military authority over the agents and operatives and watchmen or guards under his authority, and over any other persons who may molest or intrude upon any property belonging to his railroad.

Sec. 7. *Be it further enacted,* That it shall be the duty of each District Railroad Superintendent, with the aid, and, after consultation with the Presidents and Superintendents of the railroads within his district, to arrange such schedules for the movement of government trains as will insure, as far as practicable, their uninterrupted, safe and prompt continuous transportation along their several railroads, without unnecessary delays on or at the termini of either of the railroads in his district, as well as to secure like close connections and uninterrupted transportation with the railroads of districts adjacent to his own. If, upon such consultation with such Railroad Presidents and Superintendents, he shall fail to agree with them upon such schedules for uninterrupted transportation, he shall establish a schedule, to which it shall be obligatory on the officers of such railroads to conform the movements of their trains. If the officers of any such railroad, over which such schedules shall have been established, shall neglect or refuse to conform to such schedules the movement of their trains, then, upon the complaint of the said District Military Superintendent, and upon due notice of such complaint to the President or Superintendent so neglecting or refusing, the Chief of Military Transportation may, after a summary hearing of both parties, if he deem such complaint well founded, call upon the general commanding the department in which such recusant President or Superintendent shall reside, to take military possession of such railroad, and deliver it to such District Military Superintendent, to be controlled and managed by such officers as such District Superintendent may appoint, and so long as the said Chief of Military Transportation may deem necessary to the military operations of the Government.

Sec. 8. *Be it further enacted*, That, whenever transportation for troops, officers or military munitions or supplies, is desired or required by any military officer, such officer shall give the earliest practicable notice of such requirement to the proper officer of the railroad or railroads over which such transportation is to be performed, who shall himself also give the promptest notice practicable, of such requirement, to the proper officer of each connecting railroad over which the same transportation is to be continued; and any such military officer making such a requisition shall designate the hour when such officers, troops or military munitions or supplies will be completely ready for transportation, and it shall be his imperative duty to see that they are then so ready, and, after which hour no train shall be detained without the consent of the controlling officers of such railroad; but the hours of departure and arrival, and all other matters relating to the movements of trains shall be controlled exclusively by such officers of the railroads performing the transportation.

Sec. 9. *Be it further enacted*, That whenever, upon the representation of any General, commanding any Department, or in the judgment of any of the said District Military Superintendents, or of the said Chief of Military Railroad Transportation, or by a General commanding a Division, when neither of the three above named officers are present, it shall be deemed necessary, or of great importance to the public service, either to remove the rails or other movable structures, or the machinery of any Railroad in any district, in order to prevent their capture by the public enemy, or to repair, extend or alter the roadway, structures or machinery of such Railroad, or to construct any side tracks, water stations, warehouses, or other structures connected with any such Railroad; such work shall be, upon the requisition of such District Superintendents, promptly executed under the control and superintendence, if practicable, of the officers of such Railroad, and if they cannot or will not execute it as promptly or as well as may be practicable by such District Superintendent, the cost thereof in either case to be defrayed by the Treasurer of the Confederate States, on the warrant of such District Superintendent, and to be charged to, and refunded by, the Company on whose Railroad such structures are constructed, or such repairs, extensions or alterations of roadway, structures or machinery are made, to the extent only, however, and at the time when they shall be of value and importance to such Company, irrespective of their exclusive value to the Government; such value to be determined by the estimate of three impartial arbitrators, one of whom shall be selected by such Company, another by the Government, and by those two the third shall be chosen.

Sec. 10. *Be it further enacted,* That if any Superintendent or President of any Railroad Company shall wilfully fail or refuse, upon a requisition made in the manner hereinbefore indicated, to furnish transportation for troops and munitions of war to the extent required, and to the extent of the capacity of the road, the officer or officers so offending, shall be deemed guilty of a military offence, and for such offence shall be tried and punished at the discretion of a court martial—a portion of the punishment inflicted by which, should the party tried be found guilty, shall be removal from official connection with the road.

Sec. 11. *Be it further enacted,* That any officer or employee, connected with any Railroad, upon whom by this Act it is provided military rank shall be conferred, if he fails wilfully in any manner to perform his duty, as such officer or employee, whereby detention or detriment may occur in the transportation of troops or munitions of war, shall be deemed guilty of a military offence, and punished at the discrection of a court martial—a portion of the punishment inflicted by which, should the party tried be found guilty, shall be removal from office or employment in connection with the road: *Provided,* That the court martial, to be ordered under this and the preceding section, shall be composed alike of officers, upon whom by this Act rank is conferred, and of officers of the army.

SEC. 12. *Be it further enacted*, That the Military Chief of Railroad Transportation, and the District Superintendents, shall each be entitled to one Clerk, to whom shall be paid a salary of $800, except to the Clerk of the Military Chief, whose salary shall be $1,200.